Waterwheel

John Torrance

Oversteps Books

First published in 2013 by

Oversteps Books Ltd
6 Halwell House
South Pool
Nr Kingsbridge
Devon
TQ7 2RX
UK

www.overstepsbooks.com

Printed in Great Britain by imprint digital, Devon

The book is dedicated to Barbara,
and is offered as a memorial
to Jan and Charity.

This collection is in three parts.

The first part, 'Touchstone', contains poems written in 2000 and 2001 for a poet and friend from schooldays, Jan Farquharson, who was dying from cancer.

The second part, 'Still Life', contains poems from 2000 to 2006 about my wife Charity, whose progressive dementia was cut short by a fatal stroke.

The third part, 'Honeycomb' contains poems written about or for my present partner Barbara, Jan's widow.

Contents

Honeycomb

Getting the Old Mill Going Again

When the sluice in the leat is opened
the first bucket fills, and spills
down into the second, which fills
and spills out into a third, and then

the great wheel creaks and stirs
and slowly begins to move, and when
the fourth bucket overflows, it
starts to turn, and now the water

tumbles out as the wheel comes round,
falling and filling, rumbling and spilling,
faster and up again, over and down
and round and round, until at last
it turns and turns and turns and turns and turns ...

And the cogwheels of oak and applewood turn
and the oak shaft turns, and the millstone now
goes round and round on the stone below
and the grain between them is ground to flour
which falls in the hopper and fills the sacks.

Then time is up and the sightseers leave,
the sluice is shut, the wheel slows down
and stops, and the channelled force
of the leat runs off and away to the sea.

Yet it's not quite lost if you feel the kick
as a new wheel starts to turn in your mind
with a new sluice open, a fresh leat running,
and a promise of more good grain to grind.

Touchstone

Fireworks and Morphine

August, the final hours. The rainswept quay
is loud with stalls, steel bands and roundabouts.
An autumn wind dries out the waiting crowds.
It's firework time, it's summer's last display.

He'd asked if morphine made his voice sound strange.
No. But distant, low, conspiratorial,
as if an agent scouting undercover
and ringing to report, had been surprised
to find the enemy base at such close range.

The first of many bangs turns eyes to the raft,
then up: a sky of rubies, sea of claret.
Next, an effervescent silver forest
fountains up on silver-plated waves.
Smoky treeshapes drift away to the left.

I think: those sonnets, his coruscating poem,
the tough gut-labour and the formal triumphs,
hard self-redemption — all that before the gripes,
as if some sourly festering afterbirth,
jealous of a book being born, sulked in the womb.

Now comes a finale of slowly falling stars.
People clap and whistle, boats are hooting,
echoes ring around the harbouring hills.
I wonder if he — if we — will have a year,
another year, as good as this one was?

Barrack Road

Let's say her name was Désirée
since all I remember is wanting to get her undressed.
My handfuls and mouthfuls of breast,
of matt brown skin so roundedly stuffed
with resilient flesh, were never enough —
but nor would she go all the way.

Yet this was the scene, I'm sure,
of our tipsy late-night staggers back from town,
our groping and sitting down
here by the barrack gate, on a bench —
time to canoodle and kiss, in French,
then in through the guardroom door.

I'm only wittering on
to put off saying what is hard to bear,
that now, years later, I'm here
to find a hospital, hoping to track
a friend from even further back —
if he's through his operation.

Mostly he grunts. More real
to him than I am are the invisible rowels
of the vulture tearing his bowels.
Behind his eyes the inconstant light
seems all too faint to reignite
his Promethean fuel.

I'm told that he will mend,
and long to believe it, trying to celebrate,
this night, my wedding date.
But dining with my wife, thoughts stray
to wondering what became of Désirée
and what comes next for my friend.

Hurricane

Here come the big guns
out of the lull —
Whap! Whap-whap!
The whole house judders,
recoils, recovers,
withstands — again and again.

As old as me, this house,
both of us patched and mended.
Soft from my duvet, I feel
as if part of myself, my shell,
were bearing these buffets,
this whiplash of rain.

Out from my sleepless windows
the town is lost: only its lamps
turn livid the streaming night.
My thoughts fly west to a friend
and what he faces — nothing
so simple as this hurricane.

I watch the giant cedar
wave its great black arms,
its tattered enormous tragic sleeves,
like seaweed tossed in the tide.
The trunk's unmoving column
soaks up all the strain.

As old as me, or him, that tree.
But now — another day — and I feel
just the way the cedar was,
my thoughts all thrashing about
now that I'm told the worst.
Will roots absorb the pain?

Intermission

Sou'westers raging
along the coast
brought gales of tears
from you to me.
From you to me
they battered on my window.

Tears of rage
I bit back, writing
witty letters
from me to you.
From me to you
I wrote in the teeth of the wind.

Tears on the trees
glisten now, leaves
steam in the sun
for me and you.
For you and me
this bright exhausted morning.

Visiting Hooken

How much rain can a sky contain?
Year's end, for week on week
rain fell like the century's unshed tears,
though never enough for its wrongs.

But when, today, sun blinked on floods
I should have been shiny-minded —
free for a day from dulling chores,
I should have been easy and glad.

Driving high between sea and valleys
should surely have lifted my spirits.
Kodály vibrating out of the radio
ought to have given them wings.

But I was my own bad weather, thinking
of good times running down
in a square white house on the side of a hill
where I came with a doubting heart.

The nurse just leaving: *It's good today,
the sunshine's bucked him up.*
And the valley's mouth holds the sea in a smile
as if it were dreaming of spring.

Indoors, the kindly ministrations
of women. A lifetime's paintings,
newly mounted, light up the walls.
The house feels quiet and strong.

We pick out poems from the sheaves of years,
a time for harvest and judgment.
He did more living than dying that day
and I left with work to be done.

Handfuls of Sand

It won't just stop, this colloquy
with my imagined you. Subside
at most, be sad soliloquy.

Now it's up to me to write
the letters turn to monologues
like talking outwards in the night.

Some days I think the 'phone is fading,
the line between us growing longer
and you, the other end, receding.

Then comes meeting, bringing sweet
illusion of other times, and bitter
knowing those times will not repeat.

(I can't send this! My words reproach him.
The tragedy is his, not mine.
But if not poems, how to reach him?

Smooth the creases, send it.) Death
is doyen of terrible simplifiers.
What counts is love. All else, spent breath.

I watch a child at the sea's edge fling
wet handfuls of sand at the rising tide
and think *That's it, the whole damned thing.*

Night Visit

I called on you that night, my friend,
in a dark dream, and saw you rise
out of your sickbed to extend
both arms in greeting and surprise.

We kissed like comrades then and hugged
in silence, till I felt you slide
down heavily, like someone drugged
or ... yes indeed, as if you'd died.

But listening at your lips, the sound
of even breathing came once more.
Meaning to let you sleep, I found
I first must ease you through a door

to some strange child, a young relation,
who laid you gently down to rest.
I woke then, felt the palpitation
hammering inside my chest,

but thought, dreams do not prophesy,
it's not a telepathic warning,
it's not your spirit rushing by —
I dreaded, nonetheless, the morning.

*

It was memory's work: our latest
parting had been like this, with rough
kisses exchanged at your request,
a long embrace, our voices gruff

with vain regrets, provisional
goodbyes. I'd vowed to come again,
refusing to consider final
all that passed between us then.

Subconsciously, while wishes slept,
doubt was gnawing at that denial
and warning me I should accept
that 'latest' might mean last of all.

And now I know it did. Yet find,
beneath the grief I can't dispel
(so strange the workings of the mind)
some solace from that dream farewell.

Touchstone

From the bank of endless endurance
I borrowed this pebble, off yesterday's beach.
Something solid to hold on to,
pocket-size yet old as the earth.

It's shaped like a little lamp or quern
with a hollow such as tears might make
if they fell for long enough.
My thumb fits snugly there.

How warm it gets!
The smoothness of the heated stone
is tender to the touch.
So let it be my touchstone

for feeling's place in a hardened world,
for when to look with a warm eye
on the coldness of life and death,
when not to pass by.

Something Special

Dying is a special way of living he said,
and lived that special way to the very end —
cupped his dying in his hands said a friend —
which leaves us with a riddle now he's dead.

If death is held at bay by life and breath,
yet when life's over, all death's work is done,
done long before the undertakers come —
then where, between these absences, is Death?

I think he sidestepped all that reifying —
no waiting jaws, no angel, no cut thread.
Riding the pain he must have found, instead
of life or death, a way between, that special thing.

Journey to the Coast

We make our many journeys to the coast,
each one a fresh rehearsal for the last.
I tried to walk beside him, keeping faith
with things that mattered fifty years ago,
still shared. But couldn't share the hammer-blow
and gouge of pain, nor what it told him. Truth,
his own truth, freed him from the rebel child
within, and led him to be reconciled
with all his troubled loves. From the edge of sleep
at last, the wave took him with one smooth sweep.

Alone now on the shingle what I see,
this coast, is land and sea in unity,
a breaking line defining what is broken.
The slide of cliffs. The paths I might have taken,
sooner or later all arriving here.
And what I've known as life, unrolled before me,
doubles as death which reels me in. If stormy
and dark days lie ahead, there's much that's bracing
in what he's left me, much to embrace. And facing
out as he did, there's not so much to fear.

Still Life

Free to Stride

Severe cool freedoms of a blowing lane,
wild raspberries, meadowsweet and rain-swagged trees,
all to my needs. My first clear walk alone
since threading undercliff and pounding seas,
leaving a deathbed and going back again
with this memorial pebble which I seize
in my pocket now, angry for all that's gone,
sad for what's left, stronger for both of these.

Scrabbled awake today, a panic hand
pulling me into dense and nameless fears
which fog the mind that's always by my side,
I force compassion and desire to blend.
How can she bear it? What is it that she bears?
Easy for me, when I am free to stride.

Inconclusive

So many sentences started,
nothing said.
So many tears, unshed and shed,
nothing imparted.

Much faltering speech
but no way of telling
whether the catastrophe
just out of reach
was something imagined
or the real thing.

Was this a significant conversation?
Was it even a conversation?

It was all very intimate
with kiss and caress,
heads together, arms entwined,
locked in a struggle to communicate
mind to mind
some deep distress

with no success.

So all there was to share
was bafflement, love, despair
for an hour or more. And after —

laughter? Yes, a little laughter.

Dinner by the Sea

I wonder if you can understand? —
wild-eyed, pleading, creased with tears.
(Would this be speech, or speech-like sound?)
I try, you see ... with these ... and these —
shuffling and straightening knife and fork
on either side of where the dish
would come. Oh, this'll never work!
Too bad about my moules and monkfish.
And yet last night she seemed to feel
quite happy, smiled across her meal.

Outside, beyond the walls of glass
whose dark throws back the lighted bar
and silhouettes of waitresses,
there looms and flops the pallid blur
of breakers driving in and crashing
noiselessly on unseen sand.
Out there somewhere, unjust aggression,
the usual guns in an oil-cursed land.
In here, the wreck of one loved soul —
for us, enough to wreck the whole.

Talking to Pictures

Two photographs of separate provenance
in black-and-white, a period uniform
that's greyed his khaki and her brown coiffure.
Sixty years on they share a single frame —
so easy now, so painful for them once.

These parents' faces, face-high on the shelf,
draw her more and more as the world withdraws
acknowledgment and counts her out. Surely
these two at least will understand her fears
as they always did, and know she's still herself?

Standing close, she mouths a crooning whisper,
addressing them as if they were alive,
touches them at times, and tips her ear
towards the glass as if she can't believe
they haven't any kind words left for her.

Please let me in! she begs, and stands on tiptoe.
Is there a world behind the pictures? *Please?*
Then feels the frame and sadly shakes her head.
I can't come in, she tells them. Now she sees
the doorway's much too small, the space too shallow.

Calandre

Not in *our* house, surely? That sour stale whiff
        of homes where the witless old
        slump in their hellish circles —
        empty skulls and shrill TV.
So must it come to this? More when than if.

To me she'd smelt of samphire and the sea,
        chalk turf and thyme and harebells.
        But I was a fool to think
        I'd set a course to miss the maelstrom
and we, of all the world, go glancing free.

She was choosy but faithful to her perfumes.
        I liked 'Calandre' best,
        bringing to crowded rooms
        our bodies secretly undressed.
She can't smell now, but I spray her neck and sniff.

Index of Regression

Would you pass me the loaf
please? (I'm pointing in
through the hatch to the kitchen,
that's where she is.)
She peers at the tip
of my finger-joint
and looks all round it.
Over there, look where
I'm pointing! She passes
what's nearest my finger —
the pepper-grinder.

It's my teeth I feel like grinding!

Yet she often points.
Dogs — pointers — can point.
Babies point at their mothers.
Pointing's evidently
an *ur*-thing, elementary.
What requires something more —
empathy, whatever, something gone missing —
is looking with someone else's eyes
along an imagined line of sight.
So she misses the point
like a puppy that lovingly licks
your pointing finger but never looks
at the poo where it's pointing.

Now she passes the salt.

Oh, what's the point?
It's not her fault,
you oaf —
go to the kitchen and fetch
the fucking loaf!

Swimpy

I can't bear pretty brains,
all I need is a bit of weeting ...
I don't want to be the knobby cart,
it doesn't make any billy wood ...

I don't mean to be always
flounting in stankers, I can't help it ...
Things like this are so swimpy.
Better I could die!

Two languages inhabit
this house. There's no doubt
which is the more poetic, but
its only speaker can't repeat

the words her tongue invents.
Or so I thought.
And then, months later, caught,
amid syllables that made no sense,

a sentence: *It's so swimpy.*
Living beside dementia,
as with genius, often you simply
marvel at the mind's *essentia.*

Billets-doux

Reading and writing are long-lost arts,
dressing, washing, wiping all in retreat,
but folding and wrapping remain,
and sometimes come words like *I love you.*

So when among the knives and forks
I find a package of seashells
borrowed from a bowl by the grate
and wrapped in paper tissues

I take it for a love-note
composed from what's at hand
with care, and all the skill she has,
and placed where I shall find it.

But why are clothes-pegs left about
like tiny ju-jus on taper legs,
with tall oblique metallic erections
and twin-peaked heads like horns?

Perhaps they mark her walkabouts
and say *Look, I was here, and here.*
Or could they (surely not!) be coded
accusations of adultery?

What was That?

If it's over with poems
now, nothing but problems,
not really much caring
now, more like forbearing —
then what was that?

What was that narrow smile
doing, smile I know well, the remnant
of smiles that were wide once and tender,
and you now descending the stairs to me
saying *Why, it's my darling, my love!* —
what was that?

What was that long embrace
at the foot of the stairs all about,
your murmur *I love you, I love you*
and mine *We had good times together,
such times, you and I* —
what was that?

And what was my rushing upstairs
for, that storm of tears, and sitting
on the bed's edge shaking
and suddenly so much
too much to remember —
what was all that?

If poetry's gone from us, leaving
nothing but prose now, if living
as two is a way of surviving, if caring
is cant for enduring, outwearing —
then what was all that?

Still Life

She stood there while he sat
with arms around to hold her,
her arms on either shoulder,
staying like that.

At times he leant and kept
his head against her breast,
at times looked up and kissed
her cheek, or wept.

It seemed they had no words,
and a dome of stillness fell
like the shutting of a glass bell
over lifelike birds.

Prisoner in Pink

You stand by the crack of the door,
first by the front door
then by the back door,
doglike, in case it should open,
ready to make a run for it.

It feels like prison,
I know that. Pity, guilt.
Let's face it, it *is* a prison, I've
locked you in. Unlawfully perhaps.
And me too, chained to the key.

With tears now you ask me
Oh where have I gone?
I don't know where I've gone.
Perhaps you only wander off
to seek your own lost self.

Today you are wearing
that old pink mac. Have you put on
a memory, are you somewhere back
in pink-mac years, that pink-mac self again?
For a moment, for me, yes, you are.

Another Angle

Sitting here low on a footstool
I look up past chair-arm, elbow,
hand and supported chin
at features set in the firm
and gentle cast of the years.
I wish I could enter her inward gaze.

What I might from a chair call vacancy
from here looks more like wisdom,
with sadness and a dignity
from depths I've never had to dredge.
Tonight, on my footstool, I am the learner,
the callow one, awed by another life.

Suppose a prophet washed his disciples' feet,
grimy from so much following.
Handling the gnarled individual shapes,
solid and patient, on which their lives had grown,
wouldn't he doubt, for a moment,
if his or anyone's could be the only truth?

Exodus

Suddenly, like a gorse-pod
exploding in the sun, they're gone,
seeding the ends of the earth —
son, new wife and baby
gone, with goods in fifty boxes
stacked up in a dockyard.

You and I, alone now,
sit and face the sunset
like two old loving flies.
The bench has purple stains
where pigeons visit overhead
to gorge on elderberries.

The garden's very quiet.
Sometimes a maggoty apple
plumps on the uncut grass.
You line up in your lap
the long green pods of runner beans.
You won't have understood their parting tears.

White Pony

Seasons are shuffled, and a summer's day
is dealt to late October. Forest beeches,
greeny-bronze, delay their last red rage
against the wind. These trees are all old friends,
our private landmarks from another age.

Beside the track a forest pony stands
on nibbled grass, quite still, its pure white coat
warm-shining in the sun's low western rays.
Held by such mild and lambent loveliness,
and motionless like him, you smile and gaze.

Moments of heightened apprehension — they're all
we ever have, our lamps in the cave. And while
the enchantment holds, I can mistrust my doubt
that, even so reduced, your life remains
worth bearing, worth the empty stretching-out.

*

Catwalk and Stinkhorn

She came last night, strolling out of the 'fifties
(blue shining eyes, dark-honey hair)
wearing a dress she wanted me to see:
slim waist, full skirt that swung about her calves,
rich brown and gold. A dress quite new to me.

She trod the catwalk — I was the crowd —
paused on a dancer's rising step,
smiled across her shoulder into my eyes,
then twirled around and bent to admire the skirt,
smoothed it with her hands to either side ...

Love's like a fungus, named for what it shows —
stinkhorn, milk caps, fairy rings.
Unnamed, unknown, the subterranean cords
by which they feed and spread. Do love's live roots
still push up dreams inside my sleeping head?

A Book of Owls

She leafs through owls, and I recall
wet weather years ago, a sanctuary
for owls, the day she bought the book.
Her finger strokes the goggling pages —
strange, do they seem? Or half-familiar?
Oblivion, flying on silent wings,
keeps hunting down the shadow-mice
that stir in the ruins of her mind.

I catch myself at the brink of a plea:
Won't you come back to me, darling?
As if she'd taken a vow, face set
to follow through to the bitter end
some self-destroying pilgrimage,
which even now could be renounced,
and love made whole again, the house
our home, not just a sanctuary.

The dead I can accommodate
among my absentees, but not
what breeds these sad absurdities —
the presence in my present
of the absence of her past.
The years we shared, all dead to her,
live on in me, and all that's missing
mocks me with her propinquity.

She rubs the owls now — *tyto alba,
bubo bubo, otus scops* —
with segments of a clementine.
Then makes off for the sideboard
as if her life depends on folding,
over and over, a linen mat.
Yes, I recall her buying that too
one sunny day in Orotava.

Blather and Burning

Tonight she's nothing but voice
on the pillow beside me, raving
hour after hour in nonsensical
vocables, flotsam of phrases.

And I am nothing but body
in the hot sheets beside her, craving
the warm responsive sensuous weight
of body against me, about me.

Condemned to be only a voice
and compelled to be only an ear,
between our blather and burning
the night crawls horribly by.

Two Tortoises

Sheltered from the offshore wind
we bask on a sunny clifftop
like heavy-lidded tortoises,
wrinkled, silent, immobile.

Around, below and overhead
a little flock of seven pigeons
dive and climb, soar, wheel and glide,
a revel of wings on rising air.

Before us, the blue panorama
speaks so loud of apparent beauty
it makes me feel the strengthening pull
of endless dark beyond the blue.

Strokes for Sisters

Your sister-in-law? Professionally severe,
the nurse on duty scans the board.
Just making sure that she's still here.
Yes, through there, at the end of the ward.

A heavy morgue-like atmosphere.
She's propped on pillows,
no breath, no movement shows.
Now, after nearly a year,
the feeding tube's been taken out —
nothing now but morphine.
Eyes flick open, then fall shut
with no expression.
My farewell kiss makes no impression.
She'll never know I've been.

Back home, I think
What's up? Are you going with her?
for suddenly, to my surprise,
it seems that you've begun to sink,
your body bends, looks weak and withered,
with drooping lip and darkened eyes,
no interest, no appetite.

And now, confirming my surmise,
the doctor says that in the night
or later, you must have had a stroke. You too!
Then nurses come
and life's cut back to the bedroom.

When the hospital news comes through
it's almost as if you already knew.

Twilight

Twilight gathers in the bedroom window.
Rachmaninoff in a minor key, turned low,
wanders on melancholy steppes of sound,
and shadows, rising from the ground,
climb up the trees, which sway a little, like anchored ships.
I spoon soft mouthfuls between her slackened lips.

Mornings return and light up the wild plum
day after day. She lingers, but it's time to go.
No more fighting now, my darling. Come,
the battle's over. You won it long ago.

Dear emptying head, as you slip into emptiness
be like a river that joins the sea-surge,
nothing more left now for drowning or shipwreck,
just a current that fills as the waters merge.

Trampoline

Ah, can you last the long night through,
or another night, and another?
They're drawing to a close, our fifty years
of faithfully sleeping together.

Not that our bed was for sleeping only,
still less, we thought, for dying —
our trampoline for Chagallian trips
of blissful conjugal flying.

Tonight, as ever, we lie quite close
and yet you're far away
on a lonely road where night may never
again turn back to day.

No words between us, no caress,
no kisses now, but just
your fleeting breaths like hurried steps
left in a blowing dust.

Star

Three long nights, until her laboured breathing
subsided gently into sighs today.
Then came the stillness of unbreathing things.
Tonight her body's absence shapes the gloom,
dull blocks and slabs of silence fill the room.

I see on the empty pillow next to mine
not the pale peaked waxy mask of those last hours
(still beautiful to me) but the loving eyes
and smiles of many nights. My hands, though, feel
just flatness there, the pillowcase, the chill.

But as I roll away, resigned to grief,
to lying alone in much too big a bed,
between the half-drawn curtains comes the flash
of a single brilliant star. Entranced, I lie
unsleeping, and watch it slowly mount the sky.

Lost Anniversary

Looking at the last few public roses
in a dusty resort at the end of the season
I see what day it's not, the day it might have been.
Going for gold, we nearly made it.

I pull out a prayer-book and open
the Solemnization of Matrimony.
With this ring I thee wed, with my body thee worship.
Words we repeated every year.

The pages flutter. Here's Burial of the Dead.
Spare me a little, that I may recover my strength
before I go hence, and be no more seen.
Even the psalmist wasn't ready. Strength for what?

Now rooks flock in through the mist
in pairs or singly. They circle overhead
with raucous greetings, a chorus
of the unsentimental rough music I need.

Back home, solemn as a novice, I anoint
my finger, pull the worn gold ring
out of its groove, over the knuckle and off ...
The first time and the last.

I place it carefully in a small round box
of crimson leather, painted with a dolphin.
Spare me a little, for my new love's sake!
I stare at my strange new virgin hand.

Honeycomb

Vigil
For Barbara

Seeing that tower of rock which stands alone
(or seems to, for it's not yet on its own)
beyond the undercliff at the sea's edge,
I thought how it began, a hidden wedge
inside a dense ancestral bed of stone,
how that was torn apart and overthrown,
how coast succeeded coast until it stood
full in the front line where the ebb and flood
met vanquished hills, how landslip then and rockfall
left just this pillar standing while the wall
of cliffs withdrew, and how it bears and braves
the suck and batter of the shingled waves,
guarding the crashed companion by its side
whose presence still fends off the gnawing tide —
and wondered from what gifts of cause and chance
this sentry drew the strength for such a stance.

Meanwhile the music as the breakers hurled
their weight against this outpost of the world
was full of solemn shelving harmonies
more grand than sad, and in the clifftop breeze,
like the notation of a descant, high
silhouettes of seagulls stippled the sky
as paragliding on the upblown air
they gathered like a choir and waited there.

On a Teahouse Terrace

After the swell of a silver band
sad notes of a trumpet solo
drift like ash through the gardens.

All we can see from our corner table,
peering down through crisscross leaves,
is slashes of silver and scarlet,
while you, alone and apart from us,
gaze through grief at the trumpeter.

All you can see from there, it seems,
is a heart still breaking, still wanting back
your man who made things happen.
How he'd have loved the winding paths
and multicoloured plumage of this day!

Return to Hooken

It's still the house that you two loved and bought
and made your living own, and now no less
alive for you being one — no sense of deadness
anywhere, but everywhere the thought

remains, remains: this place is his place too!
Half of me feels we're trespassing, two guests
with sorrows of our own, while half still trusts
that late-unfolded friendship that I knew.

We tour the garden where you planted dreams.
The studio breathes, the maples thrive, and from
the springline down into the wooded combe
seep and sparkle unpredictable streams.

Then on the shingle beach, soothed by damp air,
we three sit scooping gemstones — brilliant, wet —
from hidden layers whose colours haven't yet
dulled down. *Oh's* he called them, tears to share.

But as we leave you seem to turn away
from my approaching kiss. Was that a dread
of partings, each small death, or had we spread
some disenchantment on that looked-for day?

Now comes your reassuring *No, too much
enchantment*. And comedy — it seemed to you
you'd leaned your head against my shoulder! Two
strange confusions, hearts that daren't quite touch.

Reality Problems

Out walking today I met an old friend —
my shadow, sidling along on the sand.
Lopsided and lanky, my friend has a problem
with walking upright, which I understand.
Ideally, he needs the support of a wall.

But when you're alone behind your eyes
it's good to be told that you're really there
by a close companion. Even obliquely,
even in outline. His peculiar flair
is to fall on everything but never to fall.

Shadow, answer me this, I said.
Why do I seem to hover all night
above my pillow, and why when I wake
am I so transparent in front of the light
that I hardly dare to look at the wall?

No answer, of course. No matter, I've found
a sturdier friend. She makes me real
by walking upright and answering back
and sharing the ups and downs that we feel.
Like a freshening breath. Like a waterfall.

Early Birds

Waking each day to semi-darkness
filled with the incomprehensible
chatter of birds, my bedfellow weeps
for her lost life — or so I suppose,
reaching back for my own oblivion.

But broken sleep is like a broken egg.
Now light is spilling slowly through the room,
preparing a beautiful stage for our bungling.
Soon I must draw back the curtains.
A meaningless prologue begins.

I make my mind a telescope and try
to focus down and away — on you,
my comforter as I am yours, walking alone
through the Blue Mountains. Are you attended
by crimson rosellas, do you paddle in forest pools?

I must be looking the wrong way round,
you seem so small, so far away!
But I can tell your brown head's making
phrases and paragraphs for someone,
someone who by default is me.

As if the remotest star of all
were the only bright spot in the galaxy!

Meeting at Max Gate

If long hills had long memories, these,
remembering the rumble of carts
and soft clop-clopping of heavy hooves,
should in their powerless hearts resent
the roar and stink of our heated tyres
racing to deadlined rendezvous.

This childless house was its own sunset,
rose-red bricks in a huddle of trees,
but the endlessly bawling bypass won't let it
forget what our infant century's like.
The garden seat holds too many famous
ghosts by far — this bank will do for us.

It feels like a garden where things return.
Perhaps we're not the only couple
here under false pretences. These two
big sarsens passing for ornaments
might be waiting out the millennia
till stones are left to close the circle.

We meet out of time with time pressing,
parallel lives that twist and touch.
Our weeks will swallow this secret hour,
moss and sunshine of which they know nothing.
But your gift of honeycomb holds the flavour —
something to chew on, sweet and rare.

The Heart Reproached

An empty car-park. Alone in my car
for a private hour that flies too soon,
I read your letter as lamps come on
at the dusky end of an afternoon.

I feel the justice, and mildness too,
of your irreparable reproach.
It's true, our lives might be transformed —
except my heart's *not up to scratch.*

Not long ago you blamed yourself
for finding friendship not enough;
it's my turn now to feel at fault
for not requiting love with love.

Age has colourable excuses —
lost the urge or *lost the knack* —
but something, honest or weary, says
the shortfall springs from further back,

that fifty years being loved and loving
have left just one desire in me,
to find and know myself at last
heart-free from love's heart-slavery.

How apt, these scenes we haunt, where Hardy
made life's ironies his study —
your heart, love lost, left unfulfilled,
and mine, by love's embrace half-killed!

Under the Churchyard Cherry

Underneath this blossom-roof
where shadowed white on white becomes
the cherry-petal sign for sun
blue sky must be inferred from white.

Overhead the stocky trunk
hubs a wheel of rafter-branches,
underframe for a blossom-mound
that lays its rim on grass and graves.

A few long-dead parishioners lie
inside this almond-scented roundhouse,
whose white confetti year by year
sheets their unconnubial beds.

Alive but grey in blossom-light,
with our roots, too, in buried lives,
we three find even less to say
than these laconic leaning stones.

For just as white contains all colours,
silence here includes all sounds
and in these graves lies every meaning.
All that can be, seems already said.

Thinking dare not run as yet
to leaves or fruit. Oppressed by whiteness,
weight of spring, childlike we cling
to the inference of blue beyond.

Christchurch in February

Yes, everything on that good day
was good in shades of grey —
the quiet sky and the rivermouth,
the romanesque arcades,
the grizzled ranks of gravestones
mailed with plates of yellow lichen,
the lumpish castle ruins.
And Mrs Perkins' mausoleum,
built with a door she could open up
in case she woke, alive inside —
that too was mostly grey.

But there were two small flames —
an orange candle-flame that glowed
in the cleft of a tree (who left it there?)
and the bright blue flame of a kingfisher
balancing over the millstream.
Yet nobody seemed to notice,
as if they were just for us, or only we
had joy enough in our hearts that day,
had woken up alive enough,
to see such tongues of fire.

Memories on Skin

Skin has its memories too
but unlike those of the mind
they've no past tense, no label attached
saying 'happened'.

My lover, for instance, was here! She came
and she went. Yet my skin
insists we're still coupled, my hands
still cupping her breasts, and my tongue
still teasing and tasting, our lips
still hungrily mingling, our legs
untangling, entangling.

My lover was here (was *here!*) Is it
clothing that clings so sweet to my skin now? It feels
like her belly and thighs.
Am I embracing just armfuls of air? No,
the whole lively length of her, surely, I'd swear,
is here, still here.

But knowing how quickly they fade,
these memories saved on the skin,
I've made this word-sprung bed
for re-dreaming them in.

Pied-à-Terre

Four flights up, but the rickety elegant
bentwood bannister gamely keeps pace with us
right to the top, passing a Malevich print
with a great wave breaking, past

pots of geraniums, ageless, undauntedly
climbing the windowpanes year after year.
Your upward tread, not tired after work now
but doubled by mine, wakes inquisitive echoes.

In your flat, the sitting-room cheeseplant nods.
The boy in the Hockney poster might wave
if he weren't enclosed in an egg of dreams.
For Helene Weigel, framed, there are no surprises.

In the bedroom Lord Krishna, many times over,
sits paired with his gopis in a dusky garden,
blue skin and white skin face to face.
They fill the wall, a tally of assignations.

Tonight we'll slumber like heavy doves
lulled by the ever-rumbling swell
of the vast hospitable city. We'll shrug in sleep
when sirens sing its casualties and crimes.

Come morning, we'll sit by the kitchen window
with coffee and croissants, bodies at ease,
consider plays and concerts, and gaze
on gleaming roofs and yellowing leaves,

the cobbled mews and the serried ranks
of chimney-pots, like fleets of dreadnoughts
North Sea bound. And give, for this outpost,
dovecote, snug and refuge, thanks.

Candle Song

Not all the candles stay alight.
Some flicker more than others,
some burn quickly, some
burn with a still and steady flame.
These are your meditation candles,
attracting and consuming
the restless thoughts that flutter in.

Outside, a roar of raging wind,
roar of the driven sea.
Inside, between the silent candles,
sleeps an impassive carven head
as if behind its lidded eyes
it knows the worst, yet dreams
in undismayed benevolence.

We've candles to light at midnight too,
kindness for timeworn bodies
caught in the finitudes of love.
And when you stoop beside the bed
to blow them out, they throw
on such full-breasted nakedness
the afterglow of slaked desire.

Especially

Especially afterwards,
after the last delicious sequelae
have eked and rippled out
between our wordless smiles, and when
at last I turn and curl, and you behind me,
thighs to buttocks, belly on back,
and I feel your arm slip round me warm
(especially then)
and hear your breathing lengthen to sleepiness,
love seems an obvious simplification,
no longer terrible,
bearing us on like the trough of a wave.

Especially tonight
when a wind that howled all day
beneath the whipping branches
heals itself to silence,
and undrawn curtains show where the moon,
from somewhere above, floats out a sheen on the ocean,
and happiness feels too deep and clear
to be clouded by fearfulness —
especially now,
with you and the sea-surf breathing in whispers,
love's like a landfall far-fetched and wonderful
after so troubled a voyage.

Pyrenean Cloud

Daybreak showed us nothing,
or nothing but a long-suspected truth —
that happiness is living in a cloud.

Not just any cloud, of course —
you need a sense of hidden heights
and valleys safely veiled below,
while what shows up beside you in the cloud
— a rough stone wall, a slender birch,
persimmons hung like orange lamps
on boughs already bare —
should promise pleasures which, while new,
are not entirely strange.

And if you're in the cloud with one you love
and she loves you, that's happiness and more!
The cloud might hide the world forever,
why should we two care a fig?

Hotel Four-Poster

When my heart lay lost like a ball in a ditch
it was you who gathered it, made me run with it,
      taught it to bounce.
And I'm glad you're here in this big bed, which
yes, I remember, the pillars and span of it,
      canopy and flounce.

But I'm sad for the other who lay here first,
sad that her life had to gutter out
      like a candle collapsing.
Though sorrow's receding now, over the worst,
I still hear the distant wounded shout
      of that lifetime's elapsing.

Gladness and sadness, the heart's contradiction
can still bleed a sepsis of guilt in the brain —
      quite needless! That past
was fully paid off, left no interdiction
on later loving. So kiss, kiss again —
      who's lucky loves last.

New Year, Full Moon

Moonlight on pebbles.
I trudge to the end of the beach
where curving cliffs close in.
They block the shingle-drift and bar my way
with a great white snout that's snorting back the waves.

Chalk rears above me now.
A warning-sign that rocks may fall
gleams like a panel of moonshine.
This pebble bank was made by storms
and storms could wash it away
but tonight it feels like *terra firma*,
strong and grounded,
and drums to the rhythm of the sea.

I look back at the snuggled lamplit village,
aware of my buried lives in distant towns
and scattered ash of a great love lost,
and think with awe, out here on shelving stones
between cliff and surf,
of the grinding down and renewing of things —
and so, with wonder, in this new place,
of this new year's new love.

Oversteps Books Ltd

The Oversteps list includes books by the following poets:

David Grubb, Giles Goodland, Alex Smith, Will Daunt, Patricia Bishop, Christopher Cook, Jan Farquarson, Charles Hadfield, Mandy Pannett, Doris Hulme, James Cole, Helen Kitson, Bill Headdon, Avril Bruton, Marianne Larsen, Anne Lewis-Smith, Mary Maher, Genista Lewes, Miriam Darlington, Anne Born, Glen Phillips, Rebecca Gethin, W H Petty, Melanie Penycate, Andrew Nightingale, Caroline Carver, John Stuart, Ann Segrave, Rose Cook, Jenny Hope, Christopher North, Hilary Elfick, Jennie Osborne, Anne Stewart, Oz Hardwick, Angela Stoner, Terry Gifford, Michael Swan, Denise Bennett, Maggie Butt, Anthony Watts, Joan McGavin, Robert Stein, Graham High, Ross Cogan, Ann Kelley, A C Clarke, Diane Tang, Susan Taylor, R V Bailey, Alwyn Marriage, John Daniel, Simon Williams, Kathleen Kummer, Jean Atkin, Charles Bennett, Elisabeth Rowe, Marie Marshall, Ken Head, Robert Cole and Cora Greenhill.

For details of all these books, information about Oversteps and up-to-date news, please look at our website:

www.overstepsbooks.com